GW01237601

Stained glass applique

Martini Nel

δελος
Cape Town

797 PB4

Contents

Delos, 40 Heerengracht, Cape Town
All rights reserved. No part of this book may be reproduced or transmitted in any form or by any means, electronic or mechanical, including photocopying, recording or by any information storage and retrieval system, without the written permission of the publisher.
© 1990 Delos
Photography by Siegfried Behm
Translated by Freda Barwell
Illustrations by Peter Ebsworth
Cover design by Abie and Jasmine Fakier
Styling done in Zaresa Steyn's house
Set in 10 on 11 pt Helvetica Roman
Printed and bound by National Book Printers, Goodwood
First edition 1990
ISBN 1 86826 123 9

Introduction

Stained glass appliqué has become very popular over the past few years and an increasing number of people are making articles using this technique, which creates the illusion of real stained glass.

Stained glass appliqué is versatile – it is suitable not only for blinds and lampshades, but also for miscellaneous articles like cushion covers, wall hangings, curtains and even clocks.

The numerous enquiries I constantly receive is proof of the fact that patterns designed specifically for stained glass appliqué are very rare. This is what led to my decision to select some patterns and, at the same time, use them in a few articles.

Plain cotton fabric is generally used for stained glass appliqué, but multicoloured fabric will also do. A dainty print may, for example, be used to represent corrugated glass, and chintz may be used for a sophisticated display. Stained glass appliqué is the ideal way of utilising leftover fabric, since small pieces of fabric in a variety of colours are needed for this technique. The nursery quilt (p. 9) was made mainly from remnants. Start with stained glass appliqué today and see how much leftover fabric you can put to good use! A bold colour combination in stained glass appliqué can be very successful, since the different colours are separated by black bias binding. There is often a room in the house where the colour scheme is not quite to your taste because the carpet, for example, does not go with the curtains – simply make a few stained glass articles in which the colours of the carpet and curtains are repeated and see what a difference that makes!

Materials

Fabric
Cotton is the ideal fabric for stained glass appliqué, although you may also use a blend of cotton and polyester. Chintz makes a lovely display, since the lustre of the fabric reflects light.

Needles
Use a thin, sharp needle (no thicker than number 8) to sew bias binding, since it passes easily through several layers of fabric. A short, medium-sized needle with a sufficiently large eye (numbers 7 to 10 – also called "betweens") is best for quilting.

Thread
You may use the following types of thread:
- Mercerised cotton thread to sew bias binding.
- Inexpensive tacking thread – but be careful not to use dark tacking thread on light fabric, since this may leave marks.
- Special quilting thread (which is strong and resists tangling) or ordinary mercerised cotton thread run through beeswax (to prevent it from tangling) for quilting.

Bias binding
Bias binding with a width of 12 mm is generally used, although sometimes wider bias binding is used for the top and bottom edges of a lampshade, for example. Either make your own bias binding (p. 8) or use ready-made bias binding.

Batting
Thick, soft batting is recommended for articles like quilts and cushions, and thinner, stiffer batting for wall hangings.

Thimble
Your fingertips will start hurting, especially when you quilt, if you do not wear a thimble. If possible, use a thimble both on the middle finger of your right hand and on the index finger of your left hand.

Glue
A glue stick (Pritt) is needed to paste the fabric pieces onto the background. This is not only a great timesaver – it also means you do not first have to tack the pattern pieces together. For a lampshade you need clear glue (Bostik) to paste the parchment and fabric.

Paper
Use tracing paper to trace the patterns. Greaseproof paper is obtainable from most supermarkets.

Pencils and crayons
A pencil is needed to trace the patterns and crayons to colour the pattern pieces. A special blue erasable pen is also available and particularly useful for tracing quilting patterns.

Preparing a design

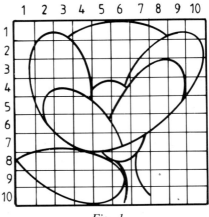

Fig. 1

For lack of space, it is not always possible to give patterns in their actual size. In such cases, only half or a quarter of the pattern is given. First trace half the pattern on paper, then turn the paper over and draw the other half on the same paper to complete the pattern. Take care that the pattern pieces join in the centre. If only a quarter of the pattern is given, trace it on paper four times.

With some articles, like the quilt (p. 9) and wall hanging (pp. 18 and 31), the patterns are so large that only a scale pattern could be given. To obtain the actual size of these patterns, proceed as follows: Draw a square around the pattern and divide it into 1 cm squares. Number the squares of the top and left rows. Draw a second square as large as you want the completed design to be. Divide this square into the same number of squares as the small square, number the squares and copy the design carefully (figure 1). Follow this procedure square by square and row by row until you have completed the entire design.

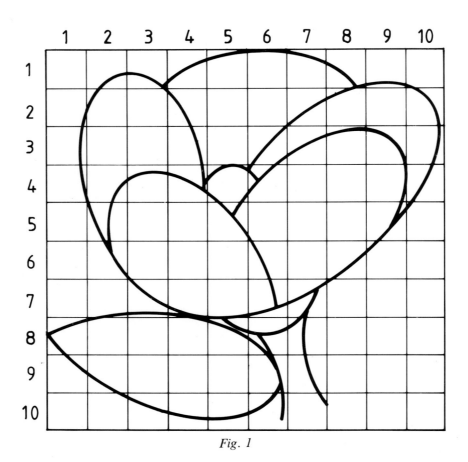

Fig. 1

Technique

Enlarge the design (p. 4) if necessary and trace it onto tracing paper. Trace the design onto another sheet of tracing paper with a black pen so that all the lines stand out clearly. Colour this tracing with crayons, matching as far as possible the fabric you intend using to ensure that the colour combination works. Number the different pieces exactly the same on both tracings. Cut out all the pieces of the tracing that were not coloured in and use these as your templates.

Cut out the background fabric to the required size and trace the entire design onto it, using dressmaker's carbon paper and a pencil. (The design may also be placed on a lightbox or stuck to a window. Stick the fabric with adhesive tape on top of the design and trace the pattern.) Number all the pattern pieces on the background fabric to correspond with the traced pattern pieces.

Trace all the templates onto the appliqué fabric or simply pin them on to save time. Cut out the pattern pieces. No seam allowances are added to the pattern pieces, since the pieces are finished with bias binding.

Paste all the fabric pieces onto the background fabric with a glue stick. You may also tack the pieces, but this is time-consuming.

Before cutting the bias binding, ensure it will not be too short – it would have to be joined to another strip of bias binding, which could look untidy. Rather cut it too long.

Close the bias binding, position it over the raw edge of each fabric piece, pin and tack it in place. Sew the bias binding to the background fabric with hemstitching or blind stitching. Ensure the raw edges of the pieces do not slip out under the bias binding. Where two pieces are adjacent, fold both edges in under one strip of bias binding.

Tip
To simplify the shaping of a curve, first sew the inside of the curve and then the outside (figure 2a).

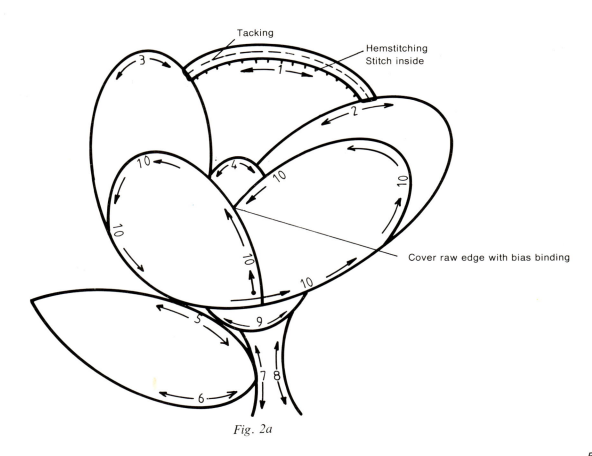

Fig. 2a

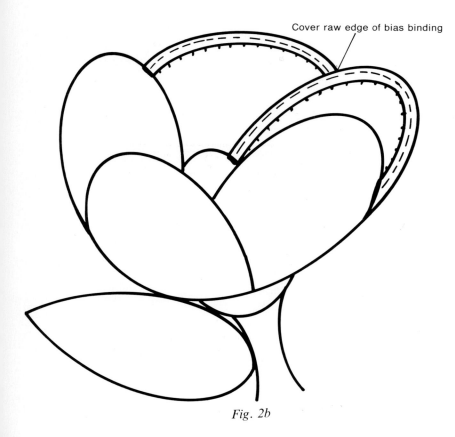

Cover raw edge of bias binding

Fig. 2b

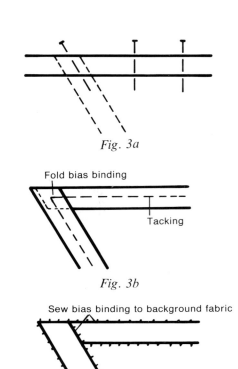

Fig. 3a

Fold bias binding

Tacking

Fig. 3b

Sew bias binding to background fabric

Fig. 3c

Both ends of each strip of bias binding must be covered by the next one so that the raw edges do not show (figure 2b). Begin therefore at the furthest point of the design or leave an opening, continue sewing and fold the end of the bias binding in later and sew down.

Sometimes, for example, when sewing the ships on the nursery quilt (p. 9), the bias binding has to be folded at the corners before you continue working (figures 3a to c).

Bias binding is usually handstitched on either side, but long, straight lines as in the quilt may be machine-stitched. This is a great timesaver, but is not recommended for beginners.

Open the bias binding and position one half over the raw edge of the fabric so that the edge remains covered when you fold the bias binding back. Sew the bias binding about 1 mm from its centre on the half covering the raw edge. Fold the bias binding back and sew the other half.

Complete the article and press it neatly. Cut off the loose threads at the back. It is now ready to be quilted. (Lampshades are not quilted.)

Quilting

Quilting consists of sewing or machine-stitching through three layers of fabric – a top layer, a layer of batting and a backing layer.

Outline quilting is generally used in stained glass appliqué. The quilting stitches are worked about 1 cm to 2 mm from the bias binding, or on the appliquéd motif or on either side of the bias binding. The quilting strengthens the article and helps prevent the fabric from slipping out under the bias binding.

When quilting a pattern like a border or a motif (flowers, hearts, etc.) on an article, trace the pattern onto the top layer before tacking it to the batting and backing layer. Use a blue erasable pen to do this. It is always easier to trace a pattern on a light box or when it is stuck to a window. Then rinse the article in clean, cold water. Do not iron the article before having washed out the ink completely.

Cut pieces of batting and a backing layer of un-bleached calico or any other suitable fabric slightly larger than the top layer with the stained glass appliqué. Place the backing layer down first, followed by the batting and then the top layer (figure 4a). Ensure there are no creases in the fabric. Tack all the layers together with tacking thread, ensuring the fabric does not fold or crease while you work. Always begin in the centre and work outwards (figure 4b). The stitching should not be more than 10 cm apart, otherwise the layers may shift or bulge.

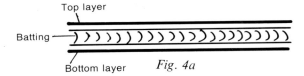

Top layer
Batting
Bottom layer
Fig. 4a

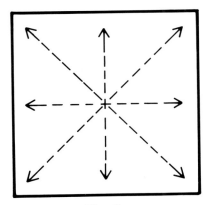

Fig. 4b

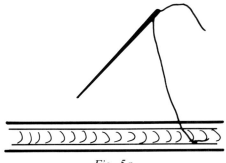

Fig. 5a

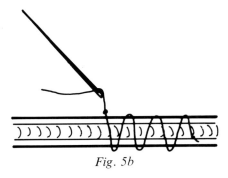

Fig. 5b

Fig. 5c

The article is now ready to be quilted. Knot one end of the thread and pass the needle through the fabric from the back to come out at the beginning of the quilting line. Pull the knot through the backing layer until it hooks in the batting (figure 5a).

Begin in the centre of the article and sew small tacking stitches (running stitches) through all three layers. The stitches must be regular and even and must show at the back. Pass the needle through the layers from the top. Hold one hand at the back of the article, feel with your index finger whether the needle has penetrated all the layers of fabric and bring the needle to the top again. Initially you will probably sew only one stitch at a time, but with practice you will be able to sew three or four stitches at a time before pulling the thread through.

To finish, pass the needle through from the back. Knot the thread close to the fabric before sewing the last stitch. Sew another stitch through the backing layer and batting only, allowing the knot to hook in the batting (figures 5b and c). Pull the thread through to the back and cut it off against the backing layer. You may also finish with two back stitches, although this is more conspicuous.

How to make bias binding

Decide how wide the bias binding should be, for example, 12 mm. Calculate the width of the fabric strips to be cut as follows: 12 mm (the width of the bias binding) and 5 mm on either side (hem allowances); the total width of the fabric strip should therefore be 22 mm. Use a strip of cardboard or a ruler of the required width to work more accurately.

Method 1
Cut out a rectangle on the selvedge thread of a piece of fabric and draw parallel diagonal lines at a 45° angle on the fabric. A ruler marked with a 45° angle will facilitate this – simply position the mark on the rectangle and draw the lines.

Draw as many lines on the fabric as possible to form a parallelogram (figure 6a). Cut out the parallelogram. Mark the points on the parallelogram as shown in the

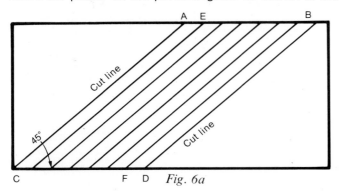

Fig. 6a

sketch. Pin the parallelogram with right sides together at C and E, and B and F. Stitch the parallelogram between the two points (figure 6b) and iron the seam open. Begin at point E and cut along the lines – this will form one long strip of bias binding.

Fold 5 mm hems on the long sides of the bias binding and iron. (Special apparatus facilitating the ironing of bias binding is commercially available.)

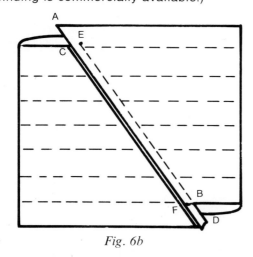

Fig. 6b

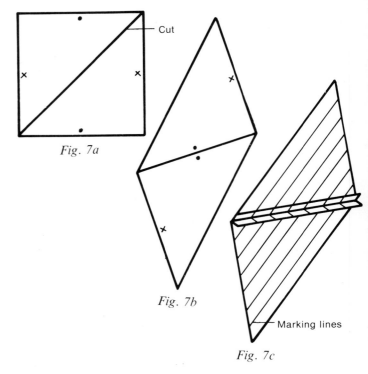

Fig. 7a

Fig. 7b

Marking lines

Fig. 7c

Method 2
Cut out a square on the selvedge thread of a piece of fabric and mark the centre of the upper and lower sides with dots. Mark the centre of the left and right sides with stars. Cut the square in half diagonally (figure 7a).

Place the sides marked with dots with right sides together, stitch (figure 7b) and iron the seam open. Draw straight lines (figure 7c) as wide as the bias binding should be, for example, 22 mm apart. Join the two sides marked with stars so that one strip protrudes at the top (figure 7d). Iron the seam open. Cut along the line to form one long strip of bias binding (figure 7e).

Fold 5 mm hems on the long sides of the bias binding and iron with an iron or the special apparatus available for this purpose.

The quantity of bias binding given under *Materials* for articles is merely an estimate and may vary, depending on how long or short you cut the bias binding.

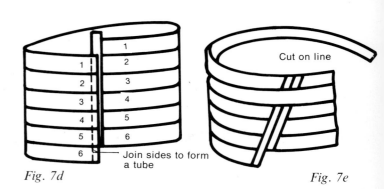

Fig. 7d   *Fig. 7e*

Toddler's quilt (about 160 cm × 240 cm)

Materials
130 cm × 130 cm background fabric
120 cm × 250 cm blue fabric
190 cm × 60 cm red fabric
170 cm × 250 cm backing fabric
170 cm × 250 cm batting
30 cm × 150 cm black fabric
remnants
2 m yellow bias binding
40 m bias binding
matching thread

Method
Enlarge the design (p. 11). Cut eight squares 40 cm × 40 cm from the background fabric. Remember to add a 1 cm seam allowance on either side, otherwise part of the pattern will be lost when you stitch the squares together.

Trace the design and complete the top layer (p. 7). Begin with the two top squares and stitch together to form a strip. Repeat this with all the other squares to form four strips. Stitch the strips together. You may also trace the design onto one big piece of fabric 80 cm × 160 cm (plus a 1 cm seam allowance right round) and complete the appliqué on the fabric itself. Then sew the bias binding dividing the squares onto the fabric. It may be more difficult to handle such a large piece of fabric but, on the other hand, you do not have to join the squares,

which saves time. Decide yourself which method would suit you best.

Cut four border strips from red fabric, two 13 cm × 80 cm, and two 13 cm × 186 cm. Add a 1 cm seam allowance on either side. Place the borders on the top layer with right sides together and stitch.

Cut four blue border strips, two 27 cm × 106 cm, and two 27 cm × 240 cm. Add a 1 cm seam allowance on either side. Place the red and blue border strips with the right sides together and stitch. The border strips may be joined, but ensure the join falls directly opposite the seam line of the squares so that they will be covered by the bias binding.

Sew the 12 mm-wide bias binding down on the seam lines and border strips. (Do not fold the bias binding over.)

Position the top layer on the batting and backing layer and tack. The article is now ready to be quilted.

Use outline quilting or quilt motifs, like birds and waves. Trim the edges of the top layer, batting and backing layer.

Cut four strips of black fabric, two 4 cm × 170 cm for the upper and lower sides, and two 4 cm × 250 cm for the left and right sides. Place the strips on the quilt with the right sides together and machine-stitch through all the layers 1 cm from the edge. Fold the binding back, fold in the raw edge about 1 cm and sew with hemstitches to cover the machine-stitching.

Toddler's quilt in detail - Photo 2

1 cm = 6,4 cm

Cushion with a fish motif

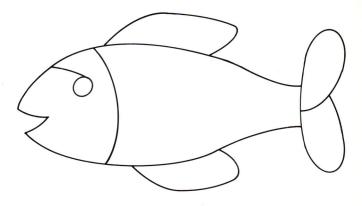

Materials
45 cm × 130 cm blue fabric
45 cm × 45 cm backing layer
45 cm × 45 cm batting
remnants
2 m piping
3 m bias binding, 12 mm wide
matching thread

1 cm = 3 cm

Method
Cut a square 42 cm × 42 cm (1 cm seam allowance included). Trace the motif onto the square and complete the top layer (p. 7).

Position the top layer on the batting and backing layer and quilt (p. 7).

Position the piping on the edge of the cushion cover, ensuring the raw edges are together and the piping faces inwards. The ends of the piping should overlap at the beginning and end. Stitch the piping down.

Cut out two pieces of fabric 42 cm × 25 cm for the back of the cover. Fold hem and stitch on one long side of each square. Place the two parts of the back of the cover on the front of the cover with right sides together and pin neatly. Stitch exactly on the stitching of the piping.

Trim the seam, turn the cover right side out, insert a loose cushion through the opening.

Cushion with a fish motif and stained glass lampshade - Photo 3

Stained glass lampshade

Materials
1 wire lampshade
parchment
background fabric
remnants
10 m black bias binding
2 m black bias binding, 20 mm wide
matching thread
1 roll of cotton tape
glue

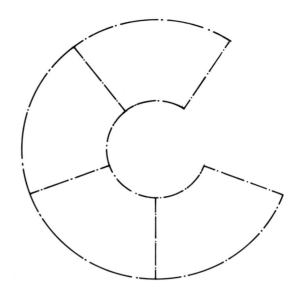

Method
Make a pattern of the shape of the lampshade by wrapping newspaper around it and cutting along the outer edges of the wire. Cut this pattern from the parchment and background fabric, adding a 2 cm to 3 cm seam allowance for the fabric.

Trace the motif onto the background fabric and complete the top layer (p. 7). The top layer is not placed on batting and a backing layer before quilting. Sew through the single layer if you prefer a quilted effect, or leave out this step if you do not.

Wrap the cotton tape around the two wires of the lampshade. Glue the parchment first to the lower wire and then to the upper wire. Use clothes pegs to keep it in position until the glue has dried.

Stretch the fabric over the parchment. Fold in the seam allowances at the back of the lampshade to conceal the raw edge and glue. Fold the upper and lower seam allowances around the wire and tuck between the wire and parchment with a sharp object. Trim the seam allowance if necessary. Paste a strip of bias binding about 20 mm wide along the upper and lower edges of the lampshade.

1 cm = 2 cm

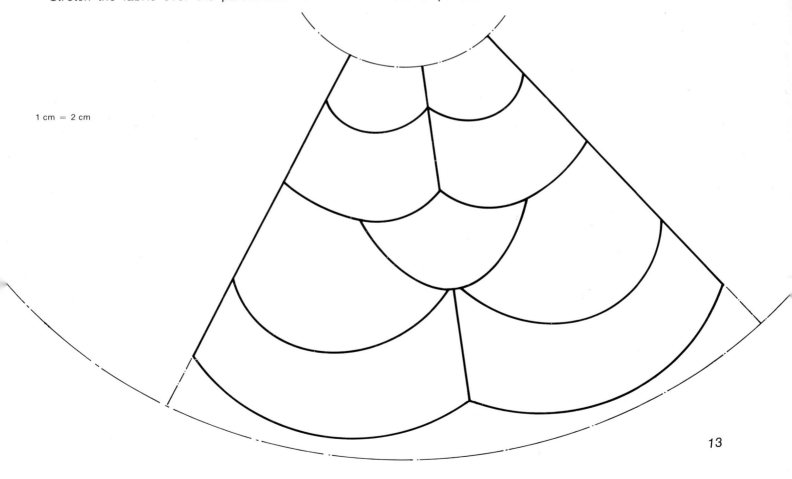

13

Square lampshade

Materials
1 square wire lampshade
parchment
background fabric
plain remnants
5 m black bias binding, 12 mm wide
2 m black bias binding, 20 mm wide
black thread
cold glue

Method
Make a pattern of the shape of the lampshade by wrapping newspaper around it and cutting along the outer edges of the wire. Cut this pattern from the parchment and background fabric, adding a 2 cm to 3 cm seam allowance for the fabric. Trace the motif onto the background fabric and complete the top layer (p. 7). The article is not quilted.

Glue the parchment first to the lower wire and then to the upper wire. Use clothes pegs to keep it in position until the glue has dried. Apply a thin, even layer of cold glue to the parchment and stretch the fabric over the parchment. Fold in the seam allowances at the back of the lampshade to conceal the raw edge and glue. Clip the seam allowances at the corners. Fold the upper and lower seam allowances around the wire and tuck between the wire and parchment with a sharp object. Trim the seam allowance if necessary.

Paste a strip of wide bias binding along the upper and lower edges of the lampshade.

1 cm = 2 cm

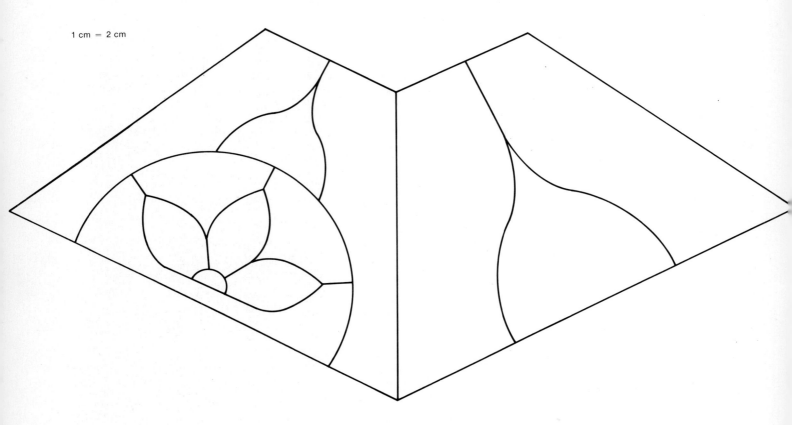

Square lampshade and clock - Photo 4

1 cm = 2 cm

Clock

Materials
50 cm × 50 cm white fabric for the top layer
50 cm × 50 cm backing layer
50 cm × 50 cm thin batting
remnants
5 m black bias binding
2,5 m lace
2 m white bias binding, 20 mm wide
75 cm elastic
1 quilting frame, 35 cm in diameter
1 circle of cardboard, 35 cm in diameter
1 clock mechanism with hands and numbers
matching thread

Method
Cut circles 50 cm in diameter from the white fabric, backing layer and batting. Trace the motif and complete the top layer (p. 7).

Position the top layer on the batting and backing layer, tack and do outline quilting. Using sharp scissors, pierce a hole through the centre of all three layers for the clock mechanism.

Gather the lace, position it on the outer raw edges with right sides together and stitch. Place the raw edges of the white bias binding and lace together and stitch. Fold the bias binding back and sew, leaving the two ends open to form a casing for the elastic.

Position the clock over the quilting frame and tighten. Using sharp scissors, pierce a hole through the centre of the cardboard circle. Fit the cardboard into the frame from the back. Thread the elastic through the casing and sew down the ends. Paste the numbers on the face of the clock, position the mechanism at the back and adjust the hands.

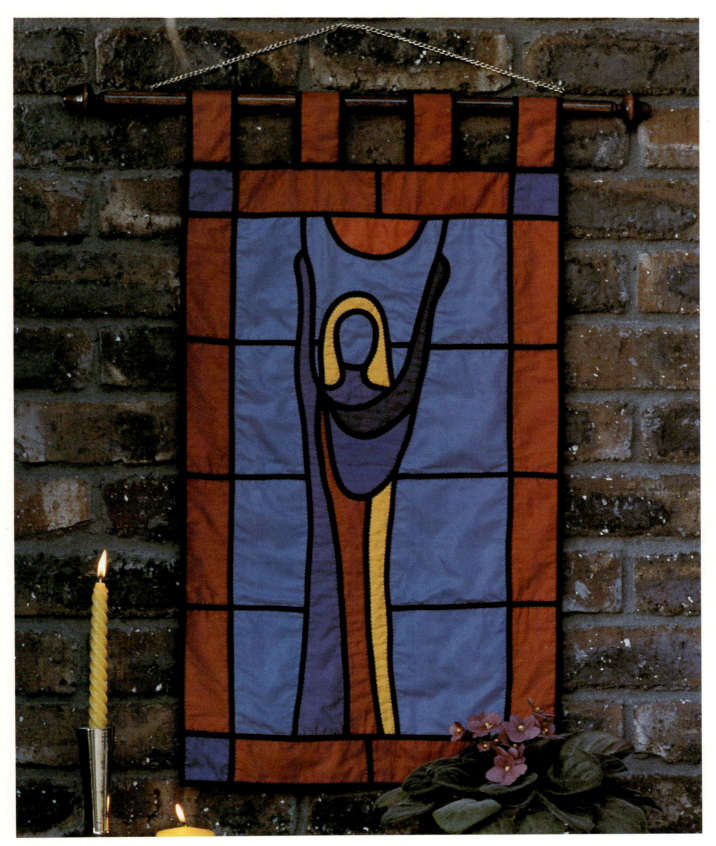

Wall hanging - Photo 5

Wall hanging

Materials
42 cm × 70 cm background fabric
42 cm × 70 cm backing layer
12 cm × 120 cm fabric for the border strips
42 cm × 70 cm batting
remnants
13 m black bias binding
matching thread

Method
Enlarge the motif and trace it onto the background fabric (p. 19). Cut border strips 6 cm wide, paste in position and divide into squares using the bias binding. Complete the top layer (p. 7).

Fold open the bias binding. Place it on the outer edge of the top layer with the right sides together and stitch. Trim the seam allowances. Fold back the bias binding on the left, right and lower sides and sew on the wrong side with hemstitches.

Cut a strip of fabric 80 cm × 8 cm and fold it in half lengthways with the wrong sides together. Fold open the bias binding and place it along the length of the doubled fabric with right sides together. Stitch the bias binding to either side of the strip of fabric. Divide the strip of fabric into four sections. Fold the bias binding back and sew with hemstitches. Fold each section in half to form the loops. Position the loops on the stitching of the bias binding stitched to the upper edge of the article (but not yet sewed to the back). Position the loops at the back of the wall hanging with raw edges even (figure 8). Stitch the loops along the previous stitching. Fold the bias binding

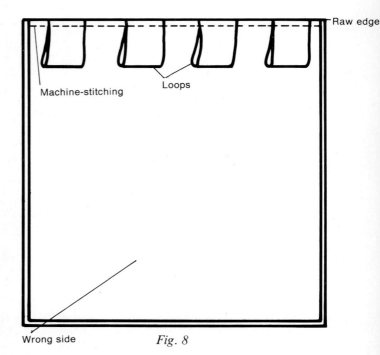

Fig. 8

back and sew with small stitches. Fold the loops upwards and sew again carefully.

Tip
You may also make the wall hanging without loops. Either make a slit for the stick at the back of the wall hanging with an extra strip of fabric, or frame the wall hanging.

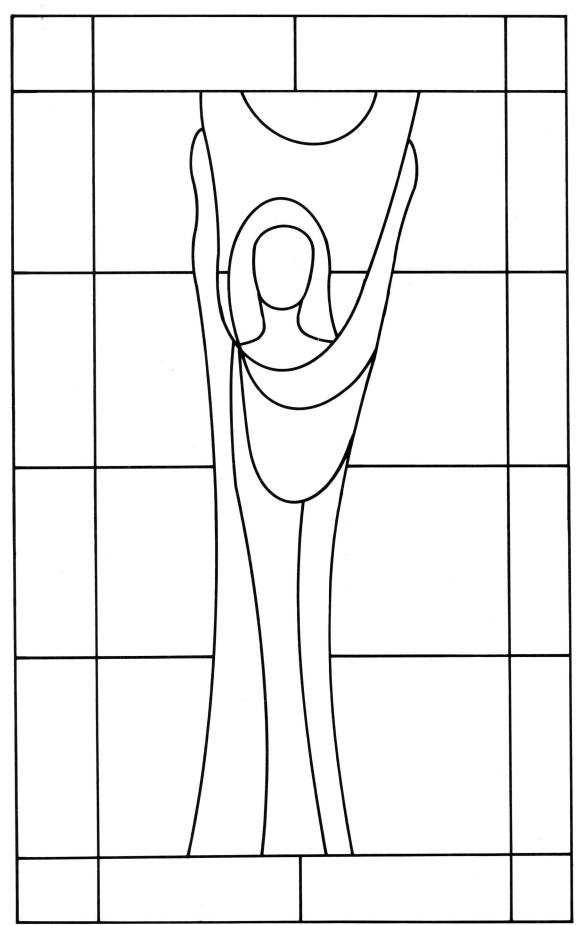

1 cm = 2,75 cm

Lampshade

Materials
1 wire lampshade (consisting of two loose wire rings)
parchment
background fabric
remnants
3,5 m dark blue bias binding, 12 mm wide
2 m dark blue bias binding, 20 mm wide
matching thread
cold glue
clear glue (Bostik)

Method
A bought wire lampshade with just two rings comes with a pattern for the parchment.

Cut the motif from the parchment and background fabric. Add a seam allowance of 2 cm to 3 cm right round. Trace the motif onto the background fabric and complete the top layer (p. 7). The article is not quilted.

Apply a very thin, even layer of cold glue to the parchment. Carefully position the background fabric with the completed motif over the parchment. Ensure there are no folds or creases in the fabric. Apply a thin layer of clear glue to the lower edge of the parchment. Begin at one end and place the larger wire on the parchment. Use clothes pegs to keep the parchment in position. Complete the lower section of the lampshade. Fold in the seam allowances at the back to conceal the raw edge and glue in position.

Apply a thin layer of Bostik to the upper section of the parchment. Insert the smaller wire ring from the bottom into the funnel-shaped lampshade so that it sticks to the glue. Use clothes pegs to keep it in position.

Fold the upper and lower seam allowances around the wire and tuck between the wire and parchment with a sharp object. Trim the seam allowances if necessary.

Paste a strip of dark blue bias binding around the upper and lower edges of the lampshade if preferred.

Stained glass lampshade - Photo 6

Multicoloured cushions

Materials (for one cushion)
45 cm × 45 cm background fabric
45 cm × 45 cm batting
45 cm × 45 cm backing layer
90 cm × 30 cm fabric for the back
16 cm × 90 cm fabric for the border
remnants
6 m dark blue bias binding
3 m wide lace
2 m dark blue piping

Method
Trace the motif onto the background fabric. Cut four border strips 7 cm × 45 cm and paste in position. Complete the top layer (p. 7).

Place the top layer on the batting and backing layer, tack and quilt.

Stitch together the two ends of the lace, divide the lace into four equal sections and mark with pins (figure 9a). Tack the edge and gather the lace evenly.

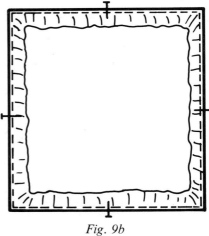

Fig. 9b

Fig. 9a

Place the lace on the fabric with the right sides together. Each quarter of the lace (marked with pins) fits onto one side of the cushion. Gather the lace at the corners more tightly, making a very small box-pleat at each corner to prevent the lace from bulging. Tack (figure 9b) and stitch.

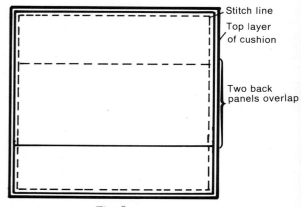

Stitch line
Top layer of cushion

Two back panels overlap

Fig. 9c

Tip
Make a double, overlapping back for the cover to facilitate taking out the cushion to wash the cover.

Cut two strips of fabric 45 cm × 25 cm. Hem one long side of each strip of fabric. Place the two back strips with right sides down on the right side of the cover front. Pin neatly and stitch exactly on the stitching of the lace (figure 9c).

Finish the seams neatly and turn the cover right side out. Insert a loose cushion through the opening.

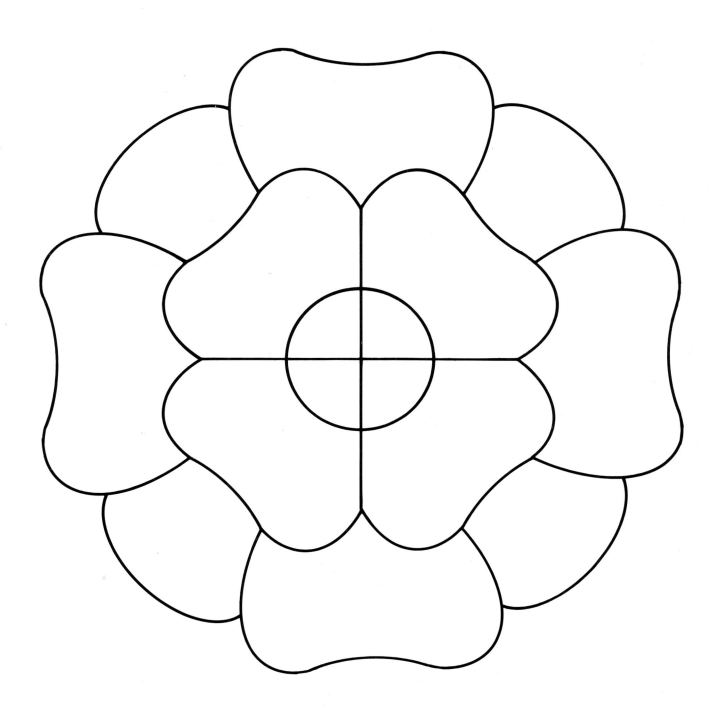

Multicoloured cushions - Photo 7

Place mats - Photo 8

Place mats

Materials
44 cm × 32 cm background fabric
44 cm × 32 cm backing layer
44 cm × 32 cm batting
remnants
6,5 m black bias binding
matching thread

Method
Trace the design onto the background fabric and complete the top layer (p. 7).

Place the top layer with right side up on the batting and backing layers, tack and quilt. Trim the corners to form curves.

Tip
Use a saucer to draw the curves before cutting.

Fold the bias binding open, place one side on the place mat with right sides together and stitch. Trim the seam allowances. Fold the bias binding back and sew with hemstitches.

1 cm = 2,4 cm

Curtain

Materials (the size of the window determines the quantities)
75 cm × 150 cm fabric (about 50 cm × 148 cm)
75 cm × 150 cm lining
about 10 m black bias binding
remnants
matching thread

Method
Either make a slit for a stick or copper pipe at the upper edge of the curtain, or make loops as for the wall hanging (p. 18).

Trace the motif onto the fabric and complete the top layer (p. 7). Cut off all loose threads at the back – the curtain will allow light through, which will show up any threads or frays.

Place the top layer on the backing layer with the right sides together. Stitch right round 1 cm from the edge, leaving an opening through which to turn the curtain right side out. Sew up the opening with small stitches.

Fold a hem of about 10 cm (depending on the diameter of the stick) and stitch. The curtain could also be finished right round with black bias binding, if preferred.

Curtains - Photo 9

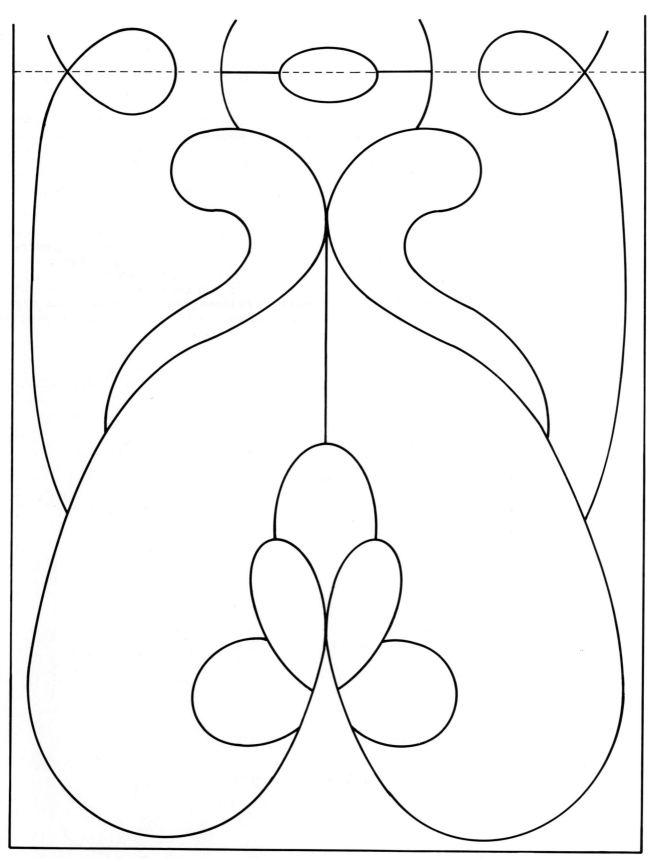

1 cm = 3 cm

Christmas wall hanging

Materials
80 cm × 70 cm background fabric
80 cm × 70 cm backing layer
80 cm × 70 cm batting
red fabric
green fabric
remnants
sequins
small strips of yellow and white bias binding
19 m black bias binding
matching thread
glue stick (Pritt)

Method
Enlarge the design and complete the top layer (p. 7). Decorate the star with sequins.

Cut a red border 7 cm wide and paste it to the background fabric around the appliquéd motif. Cut a green border 5 cm wide and paste it to the background fabric around the red border.

Stitch bias binding onto the border to form squares. Finish the bias binding at the outer edge as follows: Fold open the bias binding, place it on the article with right sides together, stitch and trim the seam allowance. Fold back the bias binding on the left and right sides and lower edge, and sew with hemstitches on the wrong side.

Cut a strip of fabric about 100 cm × 10 cm. Fold it in half lengthways with wrong sides together. Fold the bias binding open and place it along the length of the fabric with right sides together. Stitch the bias binding on either side of the strip of fabric. Cut the strip into five equal sections. Fold the bias binding back and sew with small stitches. Fold each section in half to form loops. Position the loops on the stitching of the bias binding stitched to the upper edge of the wall hanging. Position the loops at the back of the wall hanging with the raw edges even (figure 8). Stitch the loops along the previous stitching. Fold the bias binding back and sew with small stitches. Fold the loops upwards and sew again carefully with small stitches.

1 cm = 3 cm

Christmas wall hanging – Photo 10